starting with STEAM

There's MATH In My ART

Nikole Brooks Bethea

Rourke
Educational Media

rourkeeducationalmedia.com

Before & After Reading Activities

Teaching Focus:
Concepts of Print—Have students find capital letters and punctuation in a sentence. Ask students to explain the purpose for using them in a sentence.

Before Reading:

Building Academic Vocabulary and Background Knowledge
Before reading a book, it is important to set the stage for your child or student by using pre-reading strategies. This will help them develop their vocabulary, increase their reading comprehension, and make connections across the curriculum.

1. *Read the title and look at the cover. Let's make predictions about what this book will be about.*
2. *Take a picture walk by talking about the pictures/photographs in the book. Implant the vocabulary as you take the picture walk. Be sure to talk about the text features such as headings, Table of Contents, glossary, bolded words, captions, charts/ diagrams, or Index.*
3. *Have students read the first page of text with you then have students read the remaining text.*
4. *Strategy Talk – use to assist students while reading.*
   - *Get your mouth ready*
   - *Look at the picture*
   - *Think…does it make sense*
   - *Think…does it look right*
   - *Think…does it sound right*
   - *Chunk it – by looking for a part you know*
5. *Read it again.*

Content Area Vocabulary
Use glossary words in a sentence.

columns
mosaic
patterns
polygon
quilts
tiling

After Reading:

Comprehension and Extension Activity
After reading the book, work on the following questions with your child or students in order to check their level of reading comprehension and content mastery.

1. *Describe how math is used in art.* (Summarize)
2. *How can polygons be used to create art?* (Asking Questions)
3. *Where can symmetry be found in art?* (Asking Questions)
4. *Have you ever noticed patterns in artwork? If so, where?* (Text to Self Connection)

Extension Activity:
Fold a sheet of construction paper in half. Open it back up. Paint a design on one half of the paper. Fold the paper again, pressing the two sides together. When you open it, you will have a symmetrical painting!

Table of Contents

Rourke
Educational Media
rourkeeducationalmedia.com

Symmetry in Art

Look at this building. What do you see? Artists see **columns** and carvings. Mathematicians see symmetry. This means two parts are the same.

Can you point to the parts of the building that show symmetry?

A line of symmetry divides an object in half. Each half mirrors the other.

The parts match up if the object is folded along this line.

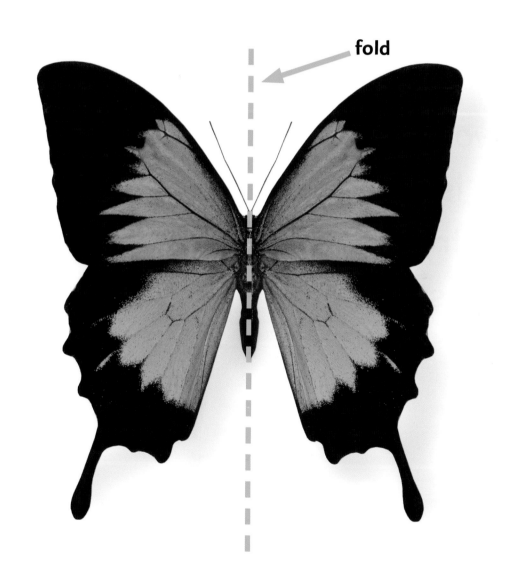

fold

Can you find symmetry in this art? There is a horizontal line of symmetry. There is also a vertical line of symmetry.

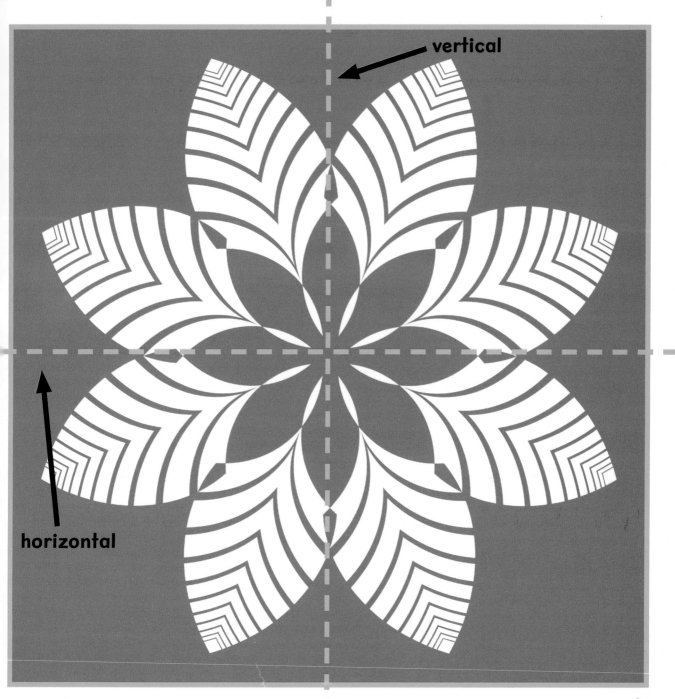

vertical

horizontal

9

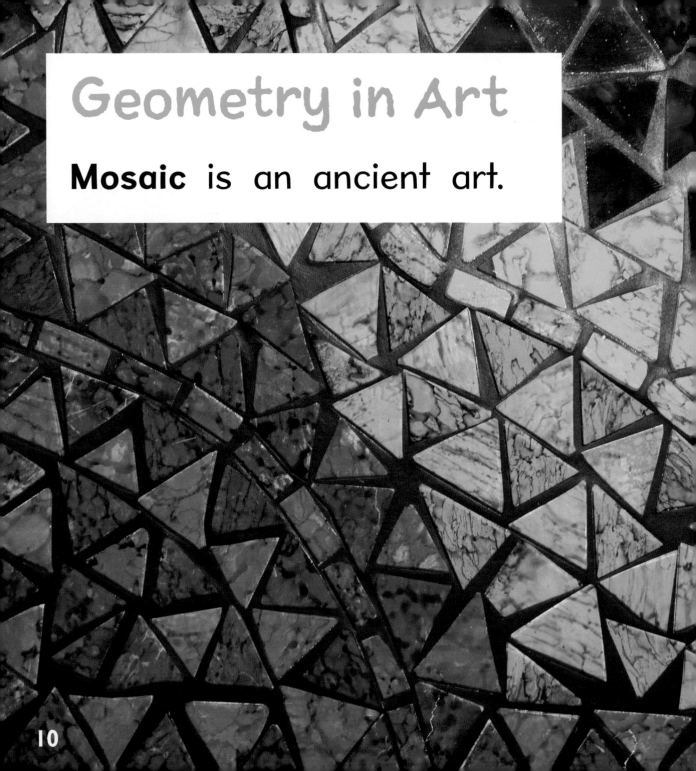

Geometry in Art

Mosaic is an ancient art.

Artists create it using tiles, stones, or glass.

Geometry is a math that deals with points, lines, shapes, and space.

Mosaic art is filled with geometry.
A **polygon** forms different designs.
There are different types of polygons

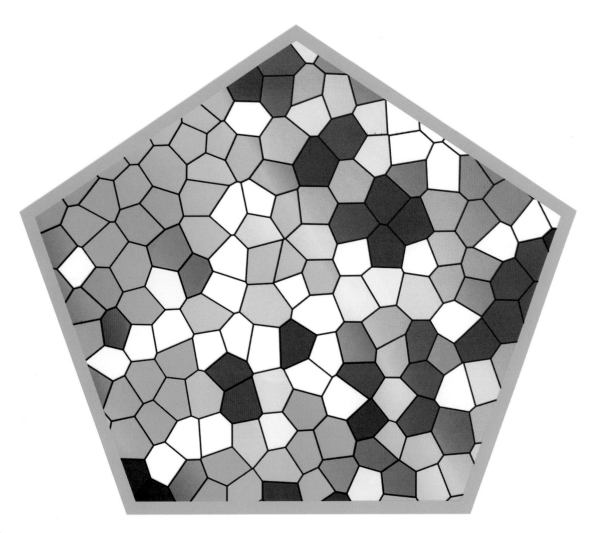

Types of Polygons

 Triangle — three sides

 Quadrilateral — four sides

 Pentagon — five sides

 Hexagon — six sides

 Heptagon — seven sides

 Octagon — eight sides

 Nonagon — nine sides

 Decagon — ten sides

Patterns in Art

Patterns repeat in art. They are found in tiles and **quilts**.

Patterns are in paintings and stained glass art too.

stained glass

A **tiling** covers a surface with repeating shapes.

There are no gaps or overlaps.

Art is all around us.

Look around. Can you find math in your art?

Make Your Own Stained-Glass Window

You will need:

- ✓ black construction paper
- ✓ wax paper
- ✓ tissue paper in assorted colors
- ✓ scissors
- ✓ clear tape
- ✓ craft glue

Directions:

1. Cut a large square, rectangle, or circle from the middle of the black construction paper. This is your frame.
2. Cut a piece of wax paper to cover the shaped hole. Tape the wax paper to the back of the black frame.
3. Cut polygons and other shapes from the tissue paper.
4. Glue the tissue shapes to the wax paper on the back of the frame, creating a pattern.
5. Allow the glue to dry.
6. Tape or hang your artwork in a window.

Photo Glossary

columns (KOL-uhms): Tall, vertical pillars that support something, such as a building.

mosaic (moh-ZAY-ik): A pattern made of pieces of colored stone, tile, or glass.

patterns (PAT-urns): Repeating designs of colors, shapes, and figures.

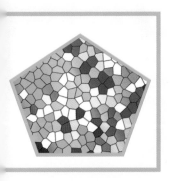

polygon (POL-ee-gon): Closed figure with straight sides.

quilts (KWILTS): Padded fabric coverings for beds sewn in patterns.

tiling (TILE-ing): The art of covering a surface with repeating shapes without overlapping or gapping.

Index

Further Reading

Curto, Rosa, *Art from Simple Shapes: Make Amazing Art from 8 Simple Geometric Shapes!*, Dover Publications, 2015.

Group Majoongmul, *Math at the Art Museum*, Tantan Publishing, 2015.

Schuh, Mari, *The Crayola Patterns Book*, Lerner Publications, 2018.

Meet The Author!
www.meetREMauthors.com

About the Author

In addition to writing children's science books, Nikole Brooks Bethea is a professional engineer. She earned a bachelor's and master's degree in environmental engineering from the University of Florida. She lives in the Florida Panhandle with her husband and four sons. In her spare time, she can usually be found at the ballfield.

www.rourkeeducationalmedia.com

PHOTO CREDITS: Cover ©Ardely, Pg 3, 4, 21 ©Dog-maDe-sign, Pg 12 & 13 ©in-future, Pg 10 & 22 ©Kalinda7, Pg 14, 22, 23 ©Ailime, Pg 16 & 23 ©Mlenny, Pg 5 & 22 ©Lightstone-Media, Pg 6 & 7 ©kurga, Pg 9 ©troyka, Pg 11 ©Webeye, Pg 15 ©nndrln, Pg 19 ©FrozenShutter,

Edited by: Keli Sipperley
Cover and Interior design by: Kathy Walsh

Library of Congress PCN Data

There's Math in My Art / Nikole Brooks Bethea
(Starting with STEAM)
ISBN 978-1-64156-424-3 (hard cover)(alk. paper)
ISBN 978-1-64156-550-9 (soft cover)
ISBN 978-1-64156-672-8 (e-Book)

Library of Congress Control Number: 2018930444
Printed in the United States of America, North Mankato, Minnesota